Gaining A.C.C.E.S.S. To Lead Others

14 <u>A</u>ctivities <u>C</u>ritical to <u>C</u>ontinuous <u>E</u>volution & <u>S</u>uccess for <u>S</u>elf

Let chemistry, confidence, and communication increase your effectiveness when leading others and being led.

Dr. Elizabeth A. Carter

© 2020 Dr. Elizabeth A. Carter

All rights reserved. No part of this publication may be reproduced, distributed, or transmitted in any form or by any means, including photocopying, recording, or other electronic or mechanical methods, without the prior written permission of the publisher, except in the case of brief quotations embodied in critical reviews and certain other noncommercial uses permitted by copyright law. For permission requests, write to the publisher, addressed "Attention: Permissions Coordinator," at elizabeth@eac-aappeal.com.

Disclaimer: The methods describe within this book are the author's personal thoughts. They are not intended to be a definitive set of instructions. The advice and strategies contained herein may not be suitable for every situation. You may discover there are other methods and materials to accomplish the same result. The author has made every effort to ensure the accuracy of the information within this book was correct at time of publication. The author does not assume and hereby disclaims any liability to any party for any loss, damage, or disruption caused by errors or omissions, whether such errors or omissions result from accident, negligence, or any other cause.

ISBN-13: 978-1-7336455-4-6

Cover Design by Purdue Designs, Macon, GA.

Back cover photograph by Russell Drake.

Publisher: AAPPEAL, LLC, Cranberry Township, PA
www.eac-aappeal.com

TABLE OF CONTENTS

PREFACE……………………………….………..v

ACKNOWLEDGEMENTS……………………….viii

INTRODUCTION…………………………………..ix

Section 1: CHEMISTRY……………………………1

      MAKING IMPRESSIONS……………...……..3

      LEAVING IMPRESSIONS……………...…....11

Section 2: CONFIDENCE………………………….15

      IMPROVING SELF AND OTHERS…………...19

      OVERCOMING INEVITABLE OBSTACLES...25

Section 3: COMMUNICATION……………………..35

      LEADING OTHERS……………………….…37

      WORKING WITH OTHERS…………….…..45

Section 4: CONCLUSION…………………….…...53

About the Author………………………….……...55

About the LEAP Series…………………….………56

PREFACE

As I was growing up, my parents embedded in me that education was important. I assumed that if I did well in school, learned a lot, and expanded my knowledge, regardless of what could happen—lose my job, car, house, spouse, or health, my education would help me get through it. Well, that is not true. I know many intelligent people with credentials who struggled, including me. My goal was to make it to the C-suite in the corporate world. I worked hard to earn excellent grades, proceeded to college, and got my bachelor's degree, but I knew it would not be enough. Every decade since then, I completed a certification or advanced degree: several insurance industry certifications, two master's degrees, and—most recently—a PhD. While that may look good on paper, it was not without challenges. My life has included

- Depending on others for transportation
- Sleeping on my mother's couch
- Moving because I could not afford rent
- Living paycheck to paycheck
- Changing careers
- Moving my aging mother in with me
- Being unemployed for 15 months

There were times when I was not sure my situation would improve, a goal required more time and patience than I expected, and I wanted to give up on my dreams. I accumulated a lot of insight from my education, but I feel that what I have achieved came from what I learned in school coupled with trial and error. Sometimes, the knowledge you have is useless or comes too late. Other times, the knowledge you need never comes. Just because you have letters after your name does not mean you know everything, and just because you do not have letters after your name does not mean you know less. It is when we use what we know and find out what we do not know that knowledge is powerful.

As we maneuver our careers, there is quite a bit of knowledge that is not easily accessible. Some of us are book-smart and some of us are street-smart, but what we all wish to be is "access-smart." The word *access* has two meanings in this book. First is the dictionary meaning: "to gain entry to or obtain." We need access to the tools and information that will help us get ahead, lead the pack, be on the top of the list, and excel in life.

The second meaning of *access* is one I created. Those who have heard me deliver a speech or training session know I love acronyms, and I try not to miss opportunities to use them. *A.C.C.E.S.S.* stands for **A**ctivities **C**ritical to **C**ontinuous **E**volution & **S**uccess for **S**elf. I want to add to your current knowledge level. You would think with all the information available on the Internet, we would all be maximizing our lives. Are you struggling to find answers?

The struggle is because not all of us have family members, mentors, coaches, leaders, or friends in our lives to share their stories with us. I have received help from many resources who shared information that became critical to my success. Sometimes, we get information before we need it, but we do not recognize it. When the lightbulb finally goes off, it is usually because we have reached a crisis and are in panic mode. The knowledge was right in front of us had we opened our minds, hearts, ears, eyes, and mouths earlier. I want to share my knowledge with you with the hope that you can use it now to set you up for future success. I offer you access and A.C.C.E.S.S. to provide the missing key to help you get your next job, promotion, or opportunity and reach that lifelong dream or goal.

ACKNOWLEDGEMENTS

I want to thank my family, friends, formal and informal mentors, and formal and informal mentees. I especially want to thank those whom I worked for, against, or with as a leader or an employee. If you read something in here and the situation sounds familiar, it was probably based on one of our interactions. Do not take it as a criticism; take it as a compliment. Thank you for impacting my life such that I could recall the situation and as its solution helped me, it is now helping others.

Finally, thank you, the readers of this book. I hope you find something among the pages that are relatable and incorporable into your life.

INTRODUCTION

STEP INTO THE CHALLENGE

If your actions inspire others to dream more, learn more, do more and become more, you are a leader

-John Quincy Adams

I hope you have read my first book and gained ideas on ways to lead yourself. You completed some of the actions and have more comfort in yourself. Now it is time to step out and lead others. Scary thought: to be responsible for individuals who are not related to you and whom you cannot control 100%. This group of people does not look like you, think like you, talk like you, or have the same interests as you. These people may not even like you. Yet, somehow, you have to get them to follow you. Most of these same statements hold true for your role when you are being led. There is someone responsible for leading you. You cannot control, speak, or even think like that person. How can we effectively survive to do and be our best every day? If you are a person early in your career, survival skills will take time to learn. For those of us a bit more seasoned in our lives, we have stories to tell and bruises to show. It is a lifelong journey and you build up some immunity to the challenges and people placed in front of you. There are situations in which everything rolls off your back, and situations that strike a part of your heart that brings you to your knees. No matter what anyone tells you, that feeling will never change. What comes with passion and purpose is pain.

As I began writing my stories to share with you, I found that some stories were relevant for those leading teams and those who were in a staff role. So, I decided to combine my themes because we all are following someone as well as formally, informally, or unknowingly leading someone else.

What is shared in this book may be familiar, but repetition confirms its importance. The topics and tips in this book are based on my personal experience. I hope either repetition, relatability, or both give you the A.C.C.E.S.S. to make changes today.

BOOK 2: GAINING A.C.C.E.S.S. TO LEAD OTHERS

When we reflect on the successes and obstacles in our journey of life, there are a few key elements that consistently contributed to the results. After evaluating my journey so far, three key elements arose: chemistry, confidence, and communication. When these are in alignment, the days are joyous and motivating. When I feel like I am failing, finding the root cause is a priority, and the analysis always leads back to one (or more) of the three. They are somewhat connected but work in an upward manner. The chemistry of interactions can make or break one's confidence, and without confidence, communication up, down, or across can be difficult. The lessons I share in this book are to help you strengthen your relationship with others because we are all leaders striving to add value to and improve our organizations and the lives of others.

This time, I have gone all-out with my alliterations to provide catchy phrases to help you remember my tips and tools. The chemistry, confidence, and communication success tips in this book include topics under headings such as

- Influence Important Ingredient
- First Flush Final
- No Not Never
- Hierarchy Helps/Hurts

I wish you success in strengthening your leadership abilities.

Enjoy!

Other books by Dr. Elizabeth A. Carter

Gaining A.C.C.E.S.S. to Lead Yourself: 16 Activities Critical to Continuous Evolution & Success for Self (Leap Series Book 1)

Before you can lead others, you need to lead yourself. Gain tips and tools learning from Dr. Carter's bumps, bruises, and braveries to elevate your life.

ISBN-13: 978-1-7336455-1-5

Good Days and Bad Days: The uplifting journal

Signify whether it was a good or bad day and then proceed to write three good things that happened and one bad thing. The balance of three-to-one is therapeutic and helps lean your life towards the positive.

ISBN-13: 978-1-733-64552-2

Other books published by AAPPEAL, LLC

A Black First by Peter E. Carter

Peter E. Carter shares his journey of weathering the storms of racism and bigotry to shine as a prominent educator in the State of New Jersey.

Learn about all his firsts....

ISBN-13: 978-1-733-64553-9

Section 1: CHEMISTRY

Your value does not decrease based on someone's inability to see your worth.

-Zig Ziglar

When viewing a tombstone, we are taught that it is not the beginning date or the end date that matters but how one lived in the "–". Over the course of our lives, we have many dashes by way of people we meet. Quite often, we do not remember anything except for the first time we met each other and the legacy left when our relationship ended. At work, we are taught to be cordial to each other, but sometimes, that emotion seems forced. I have had people try to become my friend because it was the right thing to do. Being an introvert, I only allow people whom I trust and who feel genuine to me into my circle. I have had managers, coworkers, and other employees who wanted to have coffee once a month, would come by desk unnecessarily to see how I was doing, or would invite me to their home for events. Those whom I had an immediate connection with earned their way into my circle, and they are lifelong friends whom I cherish. The invitations that I felt had some alternative motive got a polite, "Sorry, I already have plans. Maybe next time."

Those personal first impressions become clues when you are exploring new opportunities. Whether it be a new job, city, or career, there are some subliminal clues that we may dismiss, but hindsight is always 20/20. How we handle those clues is crucial, and how we leave a last impression is more important and memorable.

.

MAKING IMPRESSIONS

Be yourself. Everyone else is already taken

—Oscar Wilde

Korn Ferry recently published an article that stated there is some good news about how authentic job candidates are during the interview process.[i] Only 7% said they portrayed themselves as different than they were with the hope of landing a role. This means that people are genuinely themselves when you first meet them. You must discern whether you like the person presenting themselves to you enough to want to work with them, work for them, or have them work for you. I have made the mistake many times in saying to myself, "It will be different once he/she/I start working there." Then, when a relationship is not proceeding to change like I hoped, I admit that I saw signs earlier. What we must do at that time is analyze the situation to determine the level of discomfort. Can you brush it off like a piece of dust? Is it something that a few sips of wine on the weekend can cure? Has it caused you to buy a gym membership with a punching bag to work out your aggression? Has it required a trip to a doctor with medications being prescribed? Has it landed you in the emergency room? Whenever there is a news story of an active shooter in an office building, reporters interview the shooter's neighbors and there is always one who says, "He was such a nice man. I would have never thought he would do this," and another person who is not surprised.

The difference is about observation and noticing small clues. Following, I share some observations that can help you in your initial interactions with others. The impressions from these interactions become ingrained and are sometimes hard to shake.

First Flush Final

The phrase, "First Flush Final," came to me in 2019 and as I reflected on several employees and managers I had. I laughed about it because it is so true. People show up as their true selves during your first meeting with them. They show you their true hand, their true colors, and their true idiosyncrasies. No matter what you think, that is their final showing. Do not expect much change in their tone, attitude, humor, posture, personality, or perfume unless there is some major event in their lives by which they are profoundly mentally, spiritually, or emotionally affected.

You can usually tell within the first few minutes if your chemistry is going to be positive or negative. The exchange of first sentences have been the determining factor for me. I had a meeting once with a person, and when I walked in, the person grimaced. I did not know if the face was because I was Black, pretty, well dressed, or 5 minutes late. After that, the meeting went downhill. Maybe the person had a situation on his end that morning and it had nothing to do with me, but as professionals, we are supposed to act in a professional way.

Activity 1: Analyze the interaction and determine to hold or fold

After you have had a first meeting with someone, analyze the "cards" the person showed you. How did the person answer your questions? What was the physical and vocal demeanor when doing so? What types of questions did the person ask you? All questions are posed for a reason. Did you give a true answer or a political answer? Listening and reading between the lines is key. Do not assume the other person is bluffing. Replay the meeting in your mind and make notes of the key questions.

Once you have evaluated that first meeting, think about prior experiences. Have you seen similar behaviors in a previous coworker? Were you able to handle it? What did you learn from the past that would help you now? While making the final decision in pursuing employer–employee relationships in the past, did you forgo some of your more important qualities? If you really could not work past 5 pm and the job required you to be there until 6 pm, why were you mad when your boss reprimanded you for not getting the work done? That was lack of communication from both parties. Your manager probably asked about how flexible you were with your schedule and you probably said, "No problem." Neither of you were specific in your needs or limitations. That is some of the problem in trying to assess the hand that was dealt to you. You have the chance to change this outcome.

When contemplating the future, an important question to ask yourself is how often you will be interacting with this person. If this person is your boss or is going to be working for you, most likely, you will be interacting daily. If it is your boss's boss or a peer in another department, frequency could be less but the interaction could be especially important when it occurs. Always remember that there is something to be learned from everyone. Is there an aspect of the person's background or past or present role that could be used to your benefit? Is this person in a position where you want to be in the future? If you have contacts, or contacts of contacts, ask them about the person. When I am pursuing a new role within my company, I have done that and it always proved beneficial. People are honest, even with those they may not know well. We are all kind to offer opinions about previous good and bad leaders and employees. When you are an outsider with no inside contacts, you must really listen and read between the lines.

If you can truly work around initial areas of concern and recognize opportunities for growth, knowledge enhancement, and positive movement towards your goals, then you will allow the chemistry to be positive and flourish. If you are not sure, have another conversation with the person. This will require confidence for many reasons. You run the risk of the conversation not going well. You may no longer be in the running for the job. You could get hired and there may be some tension between you and the person. Or the person respects you for clarifying his or her position on a topic and you both have an understanding going forward. If you play your cards right, you will always have a winning hand.

Tone Tells Truth?

Along with reading between the lines is listening to tone. Tone is about the use of voice, but it can be the use of body also. I have been in meetings in which a person speaks in a loud, condescending tone accompanied by a forward lean into a table. In some settings, that person would be called "passionate" and "really attached to the project/mission/conversation." This person is celebrated. The same scenario with a different person would be labeled "aggressive" and that person would be reprimanded. The others in the meeting scurry off scared either way because they do not know if they should take the rant personally or shrug it off as the person's having a bad day. Because I listen to everything, for some reason, I hear little personal digs in those rants (maybe I am thinking too much), whereas others brush it off as a global comment. I have had to approach leaders later to check my suspicion, because once I jump to a conclusion, that first flush scenario kicks in and I start to doubt my decision about why I am there and the goals I am trying to achieve.

It is funny (well, actually sad and confusing) that one-on-one meetings are always so much nicer, never with yelling or temper tantrums, and are usually apologetic and never include a direct comment about me (though once I had to check a leader and he had no idea that what he said offended me, and after that we were the best of friends!). That is why I do not know why yelling and screaming are endorsed; it creates a mixed message and establishes a tone that can leave a lasting impression. A speaker can become a person that people love or fear. How do you want to be perceived?

Activity 2: Check your tone and whom you are talking to

I never dismiss anything I hear and do my best to treat everyone with respect. I learned a long time ago that the feet you step on today may be attached to the ass you have to kiss tomorrow. I am one who likes to check in to make sure I am focused on the right activities and people are happy with my work, and I observe the tone and body language of the response. I am mindful of my tone when speaking because my voice is somewhat deep and can come across as aggressive. When I am passionate about a topic, my voice is a bit higher pitched and pleasant with an underlying smile. Do you know how you sound when you are not happy? Is there a better place or way to express your emotions?

A lasting impression is also established in tone in the use of a key word: you.

I would participate in a monthly meeting and was always the first presenter. No matter what I said or how I changed my commentary based on feedback from the prior month's meeting, there was always a soliloquy right after my report. Every month, I felt like I was standing on the red carpet waiting to be shot. And the bullets never missed. I know the leader was using me as an example to educate all, so his use of *you* pertained to me and my peers. But he never waited until all of us spoke before offering commentary. It could have been that he wanted to speak while the thoughts were fresh or to ensure everyone cleaned up their speech before it was their turn. I do not know.

Because *you* can be singular or plural, it is a demoralizing word. It denotes finger-pointing, isolation, and disapproval. Said in a group setting, it is not clear if the reference is towards all, some, or one. If it is a group comment, preface the comment that way. If it really is an individual comment, save it for a one-on-one meeting. And please actually discuss it with the person.

Reflection Items

1) Think about the people you have worked with. What drew you to them? What drove you away from them?
2) Who were your favorite bosses? What qualities did they exhibit that were important to you? Did you click right away, or did it take some time for you to warm up to each other?
3) Are you a calmer or a screamer? Why?
4) Do you give generic feedback to a group? Do you save specific comments for one-on-one meetings?
5) Do you take global comments personally? Do you follow up with your leader to get feedback on your

contribution and how you can help improve the environment?

Notes
___

LEAVING IMPRESSIONS

When I am reviewing resumes, individuals who are in the middle stages of their careers still seem to communicate tasks, not outcomes. In my first book, I provided the suggestion that each person creates his or her own tracking of success. That is done by executing on projects and improving processes. This is how you get recognized and promoted. It also provides intellectual property that will be associated with you. Here are some suggestions of actions that will enable your voice to last well beyond your role.

Lay Legacy Leaves

It is not what we get but who we become, what we contribute . . . that gives meaning to our lives.

—Tony Robbins

I have several reports at different companies that were coined with my name. "The Carter Report" lived in fame because that was the only way it could be described. Although the report had a name, its creator was remembered. Leaving a department better than you found is what we all should strive to do. We should wake up every morning thinking, "How can I improve my workplace today?" Depending on the type of work you do, you may not have the time, access, or visibility to make daily improvements, but you should have a goal to leave something as a legacy upon your departure. It may be something you were tasked to do, it may be something you picked up on your own, or it may be something someone else dropped the ball on that you picked up. Regardless of how it arrived, own it from beginning to end, embrace feedback as a gift and not criticism, and ensure you don't make it too complicated that it dies once you walk away from it. There are several RIP Carter projects out there also.

Activity 3: Leave behind impactful reports and process improvements

As workers, we are in the problem-solving business. Companies need employees to solve problems to improve their performance, whether it be regarding product offerings, customer servicing, processing efficiencies, or future-thinking technologies. When we transition to something new, we inevitably leave things behind—some good, some bad. The important part is that what you have done is impactful and a decision, change, or idea resulted from your work. That is how you establish credibility, trust, and a legacy that may get you invited back to the team later at a higher position. You are constantly being watched whether you see it or not. Do your best every day.

Minutes Make Memories

What you leave behind is not what is engraved in stone monuments but what is woven into the lives of others.

—Pericles

I love coaching and mentoring others. We are all on this earth together and we must help each other. The notion of *kumbaya* and "We all love each other" is crap. Life is not fair. There are haves, have nots, and never wills. My coaching conversations consist of the other person asking me, "Why not?", "How come?", "When?", or "What can I do?" When I counsel and understand the root issue of the situation, I think about how I can help others. I can only speak from what has happened to me and try to envision both sides of the story through the words of that one person. We cannot read minds. We do not know what people have experienced in their lives. All we can do is rationalize.

I like to offer solutions when answering "What can I do?" The delivery of those solutions takes place in various venues: public speaking, training, consulting, and now writing. The feedback I receive, which sometimes comes years later, is from people who thank me for my words. Something I said enabled them to make a change, think differently, or transform their trajectory. I rolled out a business acumen training series in the early 2000s, and it was maybe 7 years and two companies later that I received a note on LinkedIn from a trainee thanking me for how helpful the information I delivered had been in his career progression. All from just spending a few hours with a group, caring about their needs, and wanting them to be successful and increase their value to the company. We all have unique experiences that we can share that are valuable to our employees, our leaders, and our families.

Activity 4: Leave behind impactful words

Maya Angelou stated that people remember how you made them feel, and that can be done in several ways. Examples include providing information that elevates knowledge, sending a thank-you note acknowledging efforts contributed to a project, supporting during a difficult time, being a mentor or coach, and giving tough and timely love. Payback may not come as quickly as recognition for reports and process improvements, but appreciation rests in the hearts of all you touch.

Reflection Items

1) What types of legacies have you left in the past? Were they good or bad?
2) What are you working on right now? What problems are you solving?
3) Most problems exist because solving them takes a lot of time and effort. Is there something you can raise your hand to assist with that will solve a problem and leave your mark?

4) How often do you say "Thank you," formally or informally?
5) Is there someone in the past that has had an impact on you today? Did you ever thank that person?

Notes
_____
_____
_____
_____
_____
_____
_____
_____
_____
_____
_____
_____
_____
_____
_____
_____
_____
_____
_____
_____
_____
_____
_____
_____

Section 2: CONFIDENCE

Human behavior flows from three main sources: desire, emotion, and knowledge.

-Plato

Plato's three sources of human behavior are what makes working with others exhilarating or frustrating. Everyone's behavior is different because of the confidence balancing these three sources. And these sources are sometimes not dependent on each other. I have met many people that had a ton of knowledge but no desire to share it. Others had the emotional connection, but it was an uphill battle for them to obtain knowledge. We must recognize our areas of strength that brings confidence and leverage that strength to gain insight and knowledge from others. That interaction can be great or difficult, some of which may be a product of the chemistry I described in the previous section. The only way we will improve ourselves and our confidence is by our interactions and recognizing that obstacles are inevitable.

IMPROVING SELF AND OTHERS

You cannot hope to build a better world without improving the individuals. To that end, each of us must work for our own improvement.

—Marie Curie

Every moment is a learning moment if we allow it to be. I am a deep thinker and analyze everything that happens to me. Did it occur by faith, luck, hard work, or accident? Is someone trying to help me or hurt me? Understanding self and the value you bring to every situation sets the base of your confidence. That confidence grows as you interact with others. Everyone has something to offer and something to learn.

Question, Question, Question

The man who asks a question is a fool for a minute; the man who does not ask is a fool for life.

—Confucius

We all work well in an environment in which we have confidence and knowledge. I believe, therefore, people leave managers—not jobs, cities, or industries. We are encouraged to think, step, and lean outside the box. All these things require asking questions. There are different types of questions. Some are meant for more detailed understanding. Some may be to challenge the status quo and impact change. Fear comes not from the question itself but rather how the person you ask is going to respond. Will there be an appreciation of the question, or will there be a scowl, sigh, or eye roll? Is the person going to say, "That's a stupid question," or lapse into a 15-minute monologue about the level of incompetence in the world (in a room of 20 people, of course)? Yes, I have experienced all these situations. These memories still stay with me. When I am asked to work on a project about something I don't know about, depending on the subject matter expert, if I am anticipating a question, I either feel fine or literally start to shake. I start to question myself as to why I am at this job, whether I made a mistake, should quit, call in sick, or say no to the project.

      How do I overcome the fear of asking questions to those who send a chill up my spine? I have not fully overcome it yet, but what I do is muster up the confidence and ask. If I anticipated the worst that could happen and it comes true, then I am a good psychic. Maybe the answer is not as rude or condescending as I expected, and I move on. In both cases, I revert to a happy place where I have confidence and knowledge and turn my attention to that until my sense of value and self-worth is revived.

Activity 5: Seek to understand

Some good advice that was given to me years ago (and I am still trying to be more consistent in doing) is to use the phrase, "Can you help me understand..." instead of starting with the word *why*. *Why* comes across as combative—like you are debating what was presented. Asking for help is more collaborative. You are recognizing that the person you are asking is an expert on the subject, and you want to assist in selling his or her message by being more informed about it. This is a learned skill that comes with practice. I admit that if I feel the words are not coming up my throat in a way that they will come out of my mouth succinctly, I do not speak. A more eloquently worded email later when I have had more time to compose my thoughts has worked well for me.

If someone asks me a question, whether it be for clarification or to challenge me, I am always polite and respond calmly (refer to Section 1 on tone). My confidence is there even if my response is, "I don't know. I'll have to get back to you on that," which is truly the right answer, but many try to overcompensate with words that make no sense.

Activity 6: Have data and know your numbers

What also helps me maintain confidence is that I try to gain as much knowledge as I can when possible. It allows me to answer my own questions with the data I have before asking someone else. Seeking to understand,

I will say, "I was reviewing the information and I was having trouble connecting x with y. Can you walk me through it?" This displays that there was some research done ahead of time, and talking it through may help not only you but also others in the room who may have been thinking the same but were afraid to ask.

All leaders should know the key metrics and numbers of their business unit. I used to have a color-coded document in plastic with the major variables we were tracking in my department. There are always many numbers being talked about in various meetings, and it is hard to remember all of them. A quick sheet helps when you are asked a question. Having it in front of you is comforting and you come across as knowledgeable, confident, and engaged in the business.

Always Adjust Attitude

For success, attitude is equally important as ability.

—Walter Scott

Zig Ziglar stated, "Attitude, not aptitude will determine your altitude." Have you worked with someone about whom you wondered every day how he or she got that job? Have you worked with someone about whom you wondered every day how he or she keeps that job? Both questions are about confidence and attitude. A person who is pleasant every day, works hard, and cultivates relationships will do well in life. A person who is always unhappy, complaining, and disengaged will become stagnant. A person may be a subject matter expert, be the solo knowledge holder of a system or process, or just hanging on until layoffs or retirement. I had an employee once who clearly did not like the job. The person came to work every day, did the bare minimum, did not seek to enhance skills, and did not post for another opportunity when it was suggested. A series of layoffs occurred, and this person was on the list. The person had the nerve to tell me that the years spent at the company were a waste. Why stay? Every minute of life is precious and not repeatable. Unhappiness is like a virus; it spreads quickly. One disengaged employee can impact a whole team. Team members can begin to question their confidence in the team, the company, each other, and themselves.

Activity 7: Join journey joyously

Ralph Waldo Emerson stated, "For every minute you are angry, you lose 60 seconds of happiness." If where you are is not bringing you joy, make a change. The journey of life is too short to not be happy. Positive thinking helps stress, decreases anxiety, and enables a longer life.[ii] How do want people to remember you? Sometimes, confidence blows up our ego to be bigger than we actually are. Sometimes, we sell ourselves short and minimize our accomplishments. Look in the mirror and check yourself. Have a daily affirmation to have an upbeat attitude and have the confidence to know that whatever the day brings, you can handle it. Reflect your thoughts in a journal, celebrate the good parts of your day, and learn from mistakes.

Reflection Items

1) How would you rate your confidence in your current role? Who are your go-to resources for questions?
2) Who are resources you avoid? What knowledge do they have that you need? How can you engage with them in a way that makes it a win–win for both of you?
3) What is your mood when you wake up? Is it a reaction to your calendar of events that day? How can you look at those challenging interactions as ones of education and development?
4) What elements of your day can you control? Do you make sure your confidence is evident during those times?
5) What can you do to become more confident? Is internal training, external training, coaching, or mentoring available?

Notes
_____
_____
_____
_____
_____
_____

OVERCOMING INEVITABLE OBSTACLES

Always remember, you have within you the strength, the patience, and the passion to reach for the stars to change the world.

—Harriet Tubman

Waking up in the morning with a positive attitude is key in setting the tone for the day. I say going to bed with a positive attitude is even more helpful because that sets how you sleep and how you awake the next day. Setting ourselves up for success is a great way to start, but be ready for roadblocks. We were hired to be innovative, solve problems, change the culture, be a trend setter, and help the company meet its aspirational vision and mission. Sounds great until you use your brain and come up with an idea that absolutely does all that. You have your proposal all set to go, you make an appointment with the leader for a meeting, you show up, make your pitch, and you hear those tones I mentioned previously and the body language isn't welcoming. Your ego is deflated. What happened? Your inner voice is screaming, "Isn't this why you hired me? Last year in my review, you said I didn't have any innovative ideas. Now I do and this is how you treat me?" But your outer voice politely thanks the leader for his or her time, the leader provides some feedback that may or may not be actionable, and you head back to your desk. If

I had a dollar for every "No" I've received, I'd be a millionaire, and I bet if one third of the leaders that told me "No" listened to me, the company would have made more money. But I digress, as I am sure many of you have been in my shoes, and following are my thoughts to share on the topic.

Don't Dwell Disappointments

We are all in the gutter, but some of us are looking at the stars.

—Oscar Wilde

I applied for a role that spoke to my passion. I knew I was not 100% qualified, but we know the statistics; men apply for a job when they meet only 60% of the qualifications, but women apply only if they meet 100% of them,[iii] which limits opportunities. I stepped out on faith, passion, sponsorship, relationships, and a well-documented resume. Making it to the second round and interviewing with several prominent leaders in the organization, I felt fairly good about the interactions. Chemistry was on the fence for some, but I was willing to work with it. It was going to be a lateral role within my company in a brand-new department and a different functional discipline for me. I knew I would be competing against candidates who were born and raised in that area. With the hopefulness that my background would lend itself as an asset to generate a different mindset and help the team not do the same thing that has been done in the past, I was not victorious. When I was told I did not get the job, I tried to be a big tough girl, but it did not work. I fought back the tears, but they came flowing. This was going to be my leap to align my passion, purpose, and position (also known as *zone of genius*; see the book *The Big Leap* by Gay Hendricks) and propel me into the lane of my aspirations. Not getting the position put me back in a state of feeling *been there done that* and that I was trying to make my mark but couldn't tell how I was doing. That was why I cried. It was not because I did not get the job. I realistically knew it was a big stretch and although companies say they embrace risk, they only do for certain circumstances and certain people. I had to accept the decision and go back to the drawing board.

Activity 8: Get over it quickly

In the newer generations, some parents believe that their child should get a ribbon whether he or she came in first or last in a race. This shields children from disappointment when they are young, but it is unrealistic when you become an adult. There is only one winner and lots of losers.

I have a 24-hour rule. Take 24 hours to get over something, because something else wrong (or right) is coming right behind it and you will have already forgotten this fiasco. People carry dead weight for years. Employees have a situation that happened 10 years ago with a person who is long gone from the company, but they still drag that memory around like a ball and chain and let it hold them back. From that point on, they are afraid to step out of their box. As leaders, we try to give such employees some leeway to grow slowly, offer support to ease their pain, and assure them that we are not the prior person (in most cases, we don't even know that person or we were the person's replacement). As leaders, we are a cheerleader during team disappointments. This is difficult because we all put a lot of time and effort into a project only to learn the direction changed, leadership changed, or the program was canceled. I recently took on a project and it feels like every suggestion I have gets shot down. Now I make it a game. It is like spaghetti: Keep cooking it and throwing it against the wall until it sticks. It may not be in the same form from when you started, but it is done nonetheless.

Opinions Occasionally Opposite

Opinion is the medium between knowledge and ignorance.

—Plato

It feels like *always* is a more realistic word than *occasionally*, but it is more like one third of the time there is agreement and two thirds of the time no one agrees. If there is not a unanimous vote on an idea, then more than likely, it is not going anywhere, but that depends on the opposers. I have learned that if opposers have a strong voice, then let it go; the opposers will influence others and/or create roadblocks for you. I have had that happen. A leader did not necessarily have my project on his priority list so when I asked for some time to bring it to the entire team, I was not added to the agenda. I was told the agenda was full. When I tried to leverage other team members to assist me, they went closed-mouthed. It was frustrating. I let it go and focused my efforts on projects and teams in which our priorities were aligned. I am not saying to give up every time, but do not come a to gun fight with a twig. You must understand which battles to take on and which ones to leave alone. But there is also a positive alternative.

No Not Never

Success consists of going from failure to failure without loss of enthusiasm.

—Winston Churchill

I do not take the word *no* as a negative anymore. *No* does not necessarily mean that your idea is useless and will never be used. For me, it means one of the following:

- Not now
- Need more information
- Need an alternative
- Need more value

I have taken a "No," added more content to it, waited a few months when thoughts, projects and people had shifted, and then re-presented it. The second (or third, or fourth) time, "No" became "That's interesting" or "What help do you need to define it more clearly?" and on several occasions, that came from the person who said "No" the first time!

Activity 9: Keep the faith

The moral of the story is keep thinking, keep asking, keep a positive attitude, put yourself in the other person's shoes, and understand what is important to him or her. Be confident that your words will resonate and that one person's trash is another person's treasure.

Reflection Items

1) Think about your last disappointment. How did you recover and how long did it take?
2) What did you learn from that event? Did it give you strength or did you succumb to defeat?
3) Every person has a hot spot. A hot spot is a topic that will get someone on his or her soapbox because there is a strong passion for it. When you are presenting a recommendation, are you appealing to that person's hot spot to have a better chance of approval?

Notes

Section 3: COMMUNICATION

Wise men speak because they have something to say, fools because they have to say something.

—Plato

My family gave me a lot a lot of guidance over the years. The most impactful guidance about communication included children should be seen and not heard; if you have nothing nice to say, don't say anything; think before you speak; and don't speak just to hear your own voice. I have carried this guidance with me, which may have contributed to my introverted nature but has proven beneficial because when I speak, people listen as I have something of value to share. Communication is a learned skill. The more it is practiced, the more natural it becomes. We are a world of emails and emojis, which can be misinterpreted. Whether you are managing from the top, middle, or up, I share with you in this section how you can more effectively get your message across.

LEADING OTHERS

A man who wants to lead the orchestra must turn his back on the crowd.

—Max Lucado

It is lonely at the top. When things go well, the team gets accolades. When things go wrong, you are to blame. We do not have a crystal ball to know how well or poorly a project, process, or person may perform. As leaders, we are focused on the tasks placed in front of us, but behind us are lots of barriers, excuses, naysayers, and haters. But those who are engaged in the team dynamic have got your back. You will still be out there on a limb by yourself, but they are close behind and have the net ready when you fall. As a leader, the messaging at the top must be clear enough that the entire organization can visualize their contribution to the goal. Depending on the size of the organization, midlevel managers are the crucial middle point of delivering that message. Following are ways to assist in that translation.

Cascade Clear Connections

Strategy without tactics is the slowest route to victory. Tactics without strategy is the noise before defeat.

—Sun Tzu

I created a workshop called *Leading Teams From the Strategy to Their Seats*. The objective of the training is to help leaders decode high-level, future-oriented vision and mission statements into operational day-to-day responsibilities that are relevant to employees. More commonly known as a *line of sight* (clear connection), research has shown that a key obstacle in executing strategy is a lack of ownership among employees. Instead of using incentives as a carrot to drive ownership, companies should take the time to create intrinsic motivation through communication. The communication should be in language to which employees can relate.

The process I share in the workshop includes identifying Metrics, Analytics, and Processes (a MAP) to convert the key words in the strategy into measurable and meaningful deliverables. Once you determine the key words from the strategy, determine how those words convert to terms used in your area. For example, in a strategy to create customer value, the key words are *customer* and *value*. Next, the question is understanding who your customers are and how you and your team deliver value. If your customers are not the end users, then you need to understand how your customers impact the end users. This may happen via reporting, fixing, or consulting. Review the deliverables your team is responsible for and check the alignment to the key words and the strategy. Lastly, know who, why, what, and how the deliverables will drive change and the implications, gaps, and opportunities that are evident.

Individuals on a team, regardless of their role in the organization, should be clear that their jobs are important and there are implications if they do less than satisfactory work.

Transparency Triggers Teamwork

An employee's motivation is a direct result of the sum of interactions with his or her manager.

—Bob Nelson

Once a leader has helped set a team in motion, intermittent messaging will be what keeps energy and engagement up. Your team should have regular meetings. A pet peeve of mine is when a recurring meeting is cancelled. There comes a point in time that the calendar item is a joke and invitees start to book other meetings at the same time. You lose credibility as a leader. There is information the team needs. There are updates on strategy, upcoming deliverables and meetings, administrative/human resource reminders to be shared. Meetings are a time for team members to share their questions and concerns. People do not like to live in a vacuum. With more work-from-home arrangements, teams spread across floors, buildings, states, and even countries, team meetings are important. The rumor mill is strong, people make assumptions with wrong information, distractions engulf minds, and engagement and collaboration become awkward.

Activity 10: Commit to meetings

Set a meeting day and time that everyone can consistently attend. It could be a weekly 15-minute call/stand-up meeting, a biweekly 1-hour meeting, monthly, bimonthly—whatever will work and the possibility of cancellation of which is very minimal. As leaders, we have a commitment to our team and to share with them whatever we know as frequently as we can. Everyone is buried in email, and important messages from the corporate office can be missed. Leaders receive these important messages ahead of time with frequently asked questions for team meetings, relevant actions for the team, and clarification for the team. Meetings are a time for the team to brainstorm ideas and submit comments and questions that may need to go up the chain of leadership.

Keeping and holding meetings on the calendar also helps with accountability. If there are required reports or action items due, employees know that they have a responsibility to update the team. If meetings get cancelled, employees may or may not prepare for them. Do not let meetings get cancelled too many times in a row or you run the risk of deliverables not being completed to your timeline or required quality.

Including extended team members also creates an additional commitment to not cancel a meeting. I include employees that do not report to me but provide me information for my role to be part of my staff meeting. Quite often, two groups are working together on assignments or we find we are duplicating efforts commissioned by different leaders. The ability to find that out sooner than later has saved a lot of time and aggravation. Assigning employees agenda items that they will lead during the meeting increases engagement, and peer-to-peer sharing can bring a group closer.

If you are on the other end of cancelled meetings, get your peers together anyway. You may not sit on the same floor, in the same building, or even in the same state, but you can meet and share information.

Engagement Enables Elevation

Pleasure in the job puts perfection in the work.

—Aristotle

The results of a 2018 Korn Ferry survey showed that 1 out of 3 people leave a job because of boredom.[iv] One might ask, if everyone is so busy and overloaded, when is there time to be bored? But I can relate to that. Every 2 years or so, I get bored with what I am doing. When I start a new job, yes, it is exciting—different, new people to interact with, but by Year 2, the regularity starts to set in. Has this happened to you? You have determined your friends and foes, you are trying to insert improvements that are not always welcomed, and because change is so fluid, you become numb to it and it becomes part of the workday. Responsibilities can become no longer uplifting and if a manager has not translated the *strategy to the seats*, employees can become disengaged. Gallup reported in their 2018 *State of the Global Workplace* that "18% of employees are actively disengaged at work, while 67% are not engaged at all"[v]

Activity 11: Overcome brain boredom with stretch assignments

I have a highly active brain, strategizing my career and checking that everything I do aligns to my future. By letting my leadership know my passions and aspirations, I have been fortunate to have been given special projects to keep me engaged. My passion for talent development has afforded me the exposure to several leaders, and that has extended into other opportunities. As employees, we do not always express our other interests to our manager for the fear that the manager may think we do not like our job. It is not that we do not like what we do; it is just that we are probably not maximizing our skills, creativity, and brain power. If you are a leader, ask your employees about their interests and what else would they like to be doing during their day. Quite often, it would add value to their current jobs or to another area of the organization. The cost to hire a new employee is a lot more than to retain one. Why companies chose to let employees walk away instead of transitioning them to a job with a better fit is beyond me. But as an employee, attitude is required, positivity gets assistance, and negativity does not (in most cases). Communication between manager and employee must be fluid, frank, and future oriented.

Reflection Items

1) Do you know how your responsibilities forward the mission and vision of your organization? How well have you transitioned that to the daily activities of your team?
2) What is your communication cadence? What is your cancellation ratio? Do you think your team has all the information they need (at the right time) to be successful?
3) Do you know the visible and hidden talents of your employees? Have you had a conversation about their other interests? Are those other interests appropriate for them to lead a project on the team or at a higher level?

Notes
_____
_____
_____
_____
_____
_____
_____
_____
_____

WORKING WITH OTHERS

Alone, we can do so little; together, we can do so much.

—Helen Keller

*C*ollaboration is a common word. We are no longer encouraged to do things alone, figure it out, nor struggle day and night to get projects completed. There is no time for that. Find people who already have the skills, bring them together, and complete tasks in one third of the time. Sounds simple, but as mentioned in Section 2, working with others can be exhilarating or frustrating. If a team is focused on the outcome, which is to create change, then collaboration is a beautiful event. Even though a team is aligned and has clarity of the *strategy to the seats*, communication of the team's efforts must be succinct, direct, and relevant. Regardless of working with paid or unpaid staff, knowledge of individuals' hot spots (passion or pain points) is a skill that is possible to master. Finding those points enables action and results.

Influence Important Ingredient

The key to successful leadership today is influence, not authority.

—Ken Blanchard

Many think that influence and motivation are the same; they are not. Motivation is a desire to do something whereas influence creates action and makes you do something specific. A person can be motivated but not do anything. Example, I am motivated to write a book because I have a desire to help others but that does not mean I will write one. I was influenced by reading about others who have written books and the way they have changed lives, and that caused me to put pen to paper.

When we are trying to deliver suggestions of change, we are probably in the motivation state. In this state, there are lots of interesting ideas, research, and best practices, but the presentation can lack the firmness of influence. This is where the chemistry, confidence, and communication of the team is important. There is a fear of failure, that the recommendation will not work, and careers will be compromised forever. We do not want to tell you what to do; we would like for you to do it. We never *ask for the sale*, so to speak, and our passive nature denies our ideas to be evaluated and pushed forward into action.

Activity 12: Sometimes you must DUMB it down

DUMB is an acronym. It stands for *D*ecode for *U*nderstanding and *M*aximizing *B*uy-in. You must know and understand your audience. The higher the level leader you are speaking to, the less detail needed, but the information you share must hit his or her hot spot.

Monetary or numerical impacts usually do the trick: "Profit margin will increase/decrease by $$n or n%. Volumes/market share will change by n%." If a leader's area of responsibility is impacted, you have caught his or her attention. I have seen presentations in which the presenter starts slow and builds to a climax. That method works with midlevel management or peers—those who want and understand the fine details. For upper leadership, the reverse works; because their attention span is short, after a few minutes of the meeting, they are already checking their emails on their phones. The main point must be given first and then drill-down into analysis. I worked for a leader who wanted one word on each slide and maybe a picture. That minimum had maximum impact; his conversation that supplemented the presentation always kept the attention of the team. They understood what had to be done and were influenced to go out and do it.

    I must supplement the preceding by saying that you also must know the background of the leaders you are addressing. Even though they are in a senior position, their comfort zone comes from their career upbringing and how they transitioned into their role. I worked for a leader who started as an engineer, and he loved seeing charts and reports in what I call *finance font* (numbers in a font so small that you need a magnifying glass to read it). My recommendation is to put charts in the appendix of the deck, and if/when a detailed question comes up, you can direct the leader to the page in the back.

Hierarchy Helps/Hurts

Lateral trust among colleagues is as important as vertical trust within the hierarchy.

—Andy Hargreaves

It is my opinion that we each have a level of authority which allows us to do our job. To name drop, carbon or blind copy others in order to get the work done creates an element of distrust and micromanagement, in my opinion. How come my name does not hold enough weight to be effective, why do I have to instill fear in another person for us to serve our customer? How come when I send a note, a person takes two weeks to response, but if I copy his/her manager on the note, I get a response in 2 minutes?

I am not completely criticizing the hierarchical nature in which many organizations operate. Sometimes, it is helpful. But I estimate that half of the time, it slows down the process. The leaders are not the ones doing the work; it is the staff. If the staff is directly contacted, a question or request will probably be answered well before the staff leader gets to it in his or her overflowing email box. I have had my hand slapped many a time for not copying a manager on a request, but to me, they do not need to be copied on every single request. If a manager's staff is currently working on other projects, I am fine with a response saying when I can expect an answer. The role of a leader is to remove barriers, but I do not consider requests for information a need for name dropping. If I have tried to motivate and influence and get resistance, then that is the time to move up the chain of command. That additional level of authority does help bring problems to the right conclusion.

Activity 13: Know when to push the panic button

When you know what is right and your influence is not large enough, then go up the chain of command. Make sure you pick the leaders for which this issue is a hot spot. If the issue is not important to them, then it will be hard to leverage them. I had an issue and reached out to the leaders who were directly impacted by it. I sent a carefully worded email featuring the impacts front and center, and they fired back quickly; it was great and just how I planned it. Caution: Do not push the panic button every time; otherwise, like the boy who cried wolf, when you really need help, no one may believe you. Keep your *wolf chips* for when you really need them: real critical problems. For intermediate problems, a moderate strategy can be used—conversations during the normal course of business, or one-on-ones with your manager.

Volunteers Value Vision

Be the change you want to see in the world.
—Mahatma Gandhi

I have been involved in volunteer organizations since my teenage years. Being part of a group striving to improve the lives of others has brought me personal joy and professional accomplishment. As a member or leader of a volunteer organization, you are participating in lending skills you are strong in, learning from others in areas in which you have less knowledge, engaging in collaborative and innovative projects, and creating change for the better.

The challenge that exists in these organizations, especially as a member of the leadership/board of directors/officers' team, is getting volunteers. It pains me when people feel that because there is no monetary compensation, their commitment and effort should be less. In philanthropic organizations, volunteers usually have a personal story that has intrinsically drawn them to the organization, but what about membership-type learning organizations? There may be a different desire a person has for joining, and it is up to the leadership team to investigate where that motivation lies and influence engagement.

Activity 14: Determine their why

With the competition of finite time against infinite activities to pursue, people make choices. Whether you are in a profit, nonprofit, or volunteer role, ask your team these questions:

- Why are you here?
- Why do you care?

- What goals are you trying to achieve?
- Why do you choose to spend your time here as opposed to somewhere else?

    There should be an alignment of these answers with the vision and mission of your organization. The root of the answers may be intrinsically or extrinsically driven. It may be a family tradition that a person participates. It may have been a recommendation by a friend, coworker, or boss. Perhaps the organization sounded interesting or they had a personal experience that drove them to the group. Once you understand the *why*, then you can assign committee tasks or roles appropriately. The activities in the "Leading Others" subsection of this section is key. Engagement can wane, and boredom can set in quickly. The difference in leading volunteers is that in this environment, the leader checks in more often and is more of a cheerleader. Assignments can fall off the priority list due to demands of paid responsibilities. Accountability measures must be put in place since there is not a process of a review, raise, or reprimand.

    I was part of a team with a member that had a full-time job of a highly technical nature. He really enjoyed being creative but could not leverage those creative ideas on the job. He joined the organization to keep that passion going and designed innovative flyers, website content, and other marketing materials that really promoted the organization in a wonderful way. He continues to be part of the team. That did not occur without a conversation about his *why* that allowed him to participate in a mutually beneficial way.

Reflection Items

1) Do you know the preferred level of detail your leaders like? Do you know which metrics are valuable to them?
2) Think about the last time you presented a proposal or recommendation to influence an audience. What was the outcome? What would you do differently next time?
3) What does your organization chart look like? Are they many solid and dotted lines? Who is your go-to person to assist with smaller complex issues?
4) How have you used your *wolf chips* (see Section 1) in the past? Did it result in your desired outcome?
5) Are you a member or leader in a volunteer organization? Eliminating the factor of being paid, what other differences have you observed as the motivational factors of your coworkers versus your fellow volunteers? How does that drive their engagement?

Notes
_____
_____
_____
_____
_____
_____
_____
_____

Section 4: CONCLUSION

Chemistry, confidence, and communication. As you read through the pages of this book, did memories of similar experiences arise? Were they happy stories or painful situations you were trying to forget? I hope the 14 activities presented in this book have provided you some alternatives to situations that may be new or common for you.

Now that you have reflected, what will you put into action? Pick two or three changes you will make. They do not have to be any of the activities in this book. Other ideas may have come to mind while you were reading. But please commit to do something. Here are some examples:

- Plan your leave-behind process, report, or philosophy.
- Say "Thank you" more often.
- Set a goal to increase (or possibly decrease) the number of questions you ask during a meeting.

Do your homework in advance so that it adds value and thinking to the conversation.
- Find a daily affirmation to recite in the morning, in the car, or even in the elevator heading to your floor. Have it fresh in your mind when you sit down in your chair to start working.
- Observe leaders in meetings. What are the words they use that make their peers lean forward to listen more intently? What visuals do they display that make eyes open wider? Make notes and see how you can incorporate them into your style and next presentation.
- Take a previous "No" response and turn it into a "Yes, move forward" response.

As I began my book, I will end the same: Step into the challenge. We cannot control what other people do, think, say, or feel. It is our role to be prepared to handle whatever situation is placed in front of us. Let chemistry, confidence, and communication increase your effectiveness when leading others and being led.

Thanks for purchasing this book. As a bonus, I have created the companion workbook in a pdf format. It is FREE for you to download. Go to https://bit.ly/3fF0g3m and start writing down your action plans!

About the Author

Dr. Elizabeth A. Carter is an insurance professional, performance improvement leader, speaker, and best-selling author. With over 25 years working in corporate settings in a financial discipline, Dr. Carter has a unique passion for financial acumen and knowledge empowerment that has provided her the opportunity to lead, mentor, and develop others in the areas of strategy and financial analysis, performance improvement, and talent development for profit and nonprofit organizations.

She is the CEO of AAPPEAL, LLC, a company branded on her four passions of leadership, engagement, analytics, and performance. She offers training programs, facilitated sessions, keynote presentations, and one-on-one coaching to help individuals and companies close the gaps between their current performance and desired performance. Visit her website at www.eac-aappeal.com.

Dr. Carter holds a PhD in education specializing in training and performance improvement from Capella University. She holds an MS in education in the same specialization from Capella University and an MBA in management from the New York Institute of Technology. She earned a BBA in marketing from Hofstra University. Further, she holds the Chartered Property Casualty Underwriter designation and is a Distinguished Toastmaster.

Facebook: https://facebook.com/eacaappeal/

Instagram: https://www.instagram.com/eacaappeal/

Twitter: https://twitter.com/@eacaappeal/

LinkedIn: https://www.linkedin.com/in/elizabethcartercpcu/

About the LEAP Series

The LEAP Series is a source of books and online and facilitated training to help individuals and organizations grow their career and business. The key topics of the series pertain to leadership, engagement, analytics, and performance.

The LEAP Series is a component of the company AAPPEAL, LLC, which is focused on closing the gaps to make you more "appealing" to your company and grow your career.

Other books by Dr. Elizabeth A. Carter

Gaining A.C.C.E.S.S. to Lead Yourself: 16 Activities Critical to Continuous Evolution & Success for Self (Leap Series Book 1)

Before you can lead others, you need to lead yourself. Gain tips and tools learning from Dr. Carter's bumps, bruises, and braveries to elevate your life.

ISBN-13: 978-1-7336455-1-5

Good Days and Bad Days: The uplifting journal

Signify whether it was a good or bad day and then proceed to write three good things that happened and one bad thing. The balance of three-to-one is therapeutic and helps lean your life towards the positive.

ISBN-13: 978-1-733-64552-2

Other books published by AAPPEAL, LLC

A Black First by Peter E. Carter

Peter E. Carter shares his journey of weathering the storms of racism and bigotry to shine as a prominent educator in the State of New Jersey. Learn about all his firsts....

ISBN-13: 978-1-733-64553-9

ENDNOTES

[i] Korn Ferry: BREAKING BOREDOM: JOB SEEKERS JUMPING SHIP FOR NEW CHALLENGES IN 2018, Retrieved from https://www.kornferry.com/press/breaking-boredom-job-seekers-jumping-ship-for-new-challenges-in-2018-according-to-korn-ferry-survey

[ii] Jude Paler (2018), 4 Science-backed benefits of positive thinking and how to do it, Retrieved from https://ideapod.com/4-science-backed-benefits-of-positive-thinking-and-how-to-do-it/

[iii] Tara Sophia Mohr (2014) Why Women Don't Apply for Jobs Unless They're 100% Qualified, Harvard Business Review. Retrieved from https://hbr.org/2014/08/why-women-dont-apply-for-jobs-unless-theyre-100-qualified

[iv] Korn Ferry: BREAKING BOREDOM: JOB SEEKERS JUMPING SHIP FOR NEW CHALLENGES IN 2018

[v] Employee engagement on the rise: Gallup survey shows increase from 2015. (2018). Retrieved from https://www.hrexchangenetwork.com/employee-engagement/articles/employee-engagement-on-the-rise-gallup-survey

www.ingramcontent.com/pod-product-compliance
Lightning Source LLC
Chambersburg PA
CBHW031421040426
42444CB00005B/662